W9-BWK-874

NOSE, TOES, ANTLERS, TAIL

NOSE, TOES, ANTLERS, TAIL

By Michael Berenstain
Illustrated by Roy McKie

CURR
PZ
7
.B47
Nos
1991

A GOLDEN BOOK • NEW YORK

Western Publishing Company, Inc., Racine, Wisconsin 53404

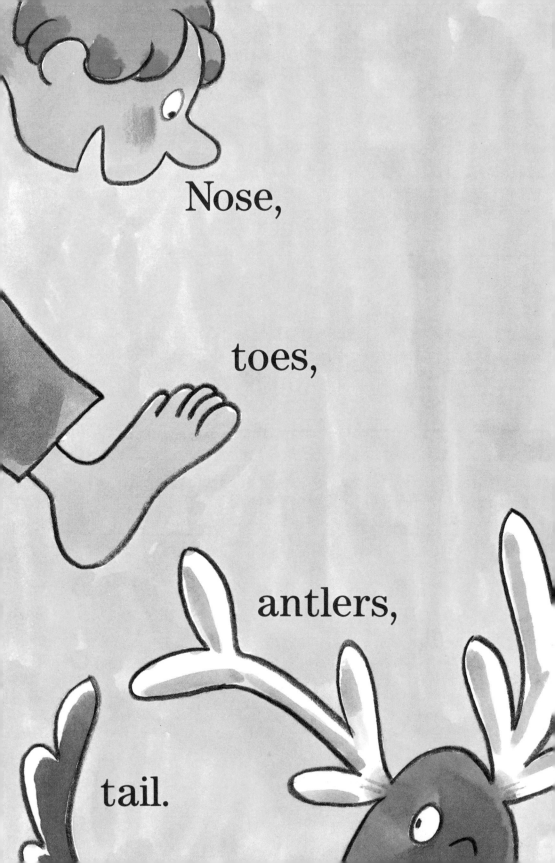

Nose,

toes,

antlers,

tail.

Horns,

hand,

fingernail.

3

Eyes,

ears,

tooth,

and
claw.

4

Adam's
apple,

tusk,

and
paw.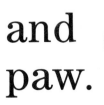

5

Eyebrows,

sideburns,

mustache,

chin.

Fur

and feathers,

scales and fin.

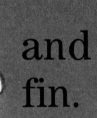

7

Stripes,

spots,

splotches,

speckles.

Mumps,

measles,

lots of
freckles.

Octopus arms,

jellyfish
jelly.

Walrus flippers,

porpoise belly.

11

A camel's hump,

or maybe two.

"Biggest mouth in the
city zoo!"

13

Gorilla muscles,

belly
button.

14

Fleecy wool,

leg of
mutton.

Bat wings,

bird wings,

robin
redbreast.

Bee wings,

bug wings,

cockatoo
crest.

Kangaroo
pouch,

porcupine quills.

Pelican pouch,

platypus bill.

19

Beaver paddle,

sawfish saw.

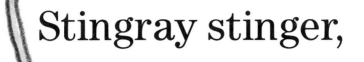

Stingray stinger,

crocodile jaw.

Armadillo armor,

turtle shell.

Hedgehog prickles,

funny smell.

Koala fuzz

and
cobra fangs.

Long white
beard

and
Sarah's bangs.

Ostrich neck,

dodo's beak.

Dragon's fire,

tongue in cheek.

Elephant's feet

and warthog's snout.

Wooden
leg

and white
whale's spout.

Swordfish
sword,

sailfish sail.

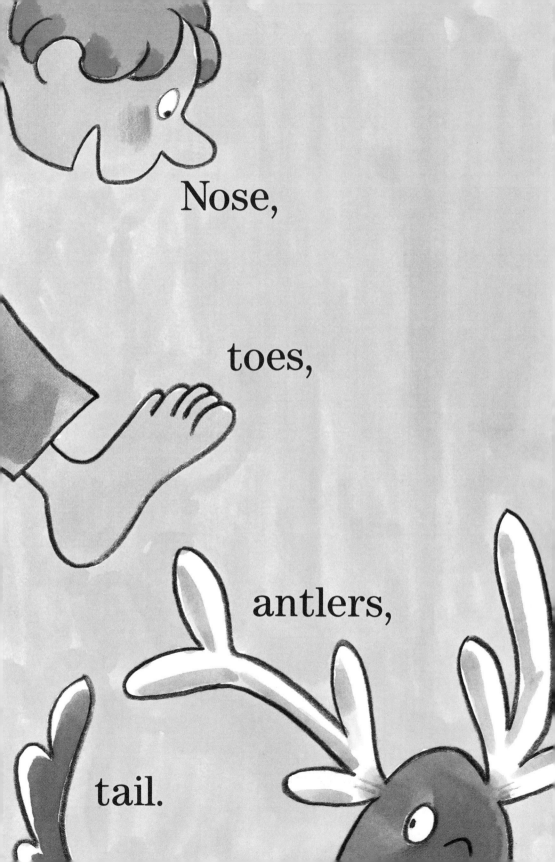

Nose,

toes,

antlers,

tail.